Valentine's Vet Visit

Practicing the V Sound

Whitney Walker

Rosen PHONICS READERS

Rosen Classroom™

This is my cat.
Her name is Valentine.

Valentine is very fast.

Valentine runs into a table.
A vase falls.

The vase hurts Valentine.

We put Valentine in our van.

We bring Valentine to the vet.
The vet is Dr. Vine.

Dr. Vine looks at Valentine.
Dr. Vine is very kind.

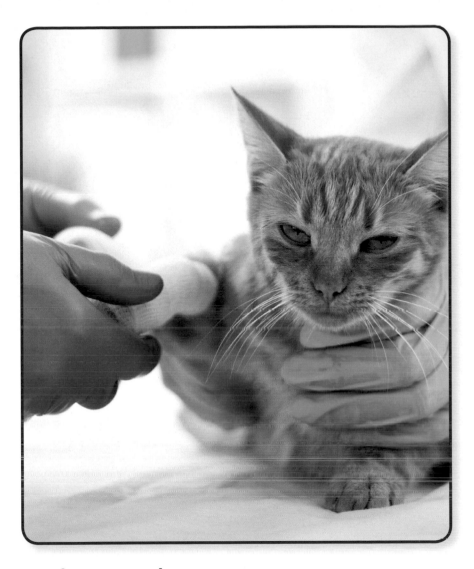

Valentine has a cut.
The vase was very sharp.

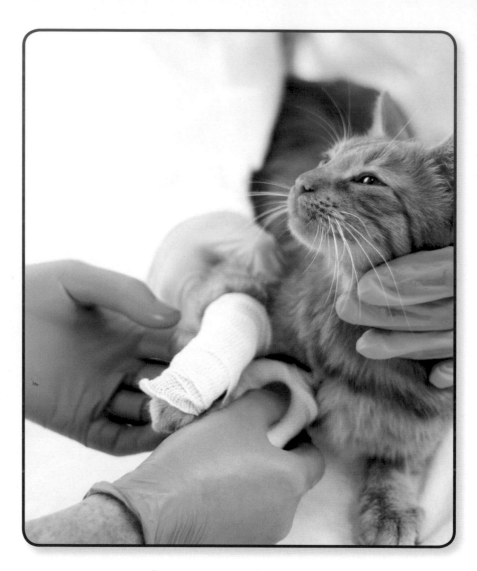

Dr. Vine fixes Valentine!

Dr. Vine is a very good vet.

Valentine loves to visit the vet!